Gershwin's
Rhapsody
in Blue

Anna Harwell Celenza

Illustrated by JoAnn E. Kitchel

Charlesbridge

Published by Charlesbridge
85 Main Street, Watertown, MA 02472
(617) 926-0329
www.charlesbridge.com

Library of Congress Cataloging–in–Publication Data
Celenza, Anna Harwell.
Gershwin's Rhapsody in Blue / Anna Harwell Celenza ; illustrated by JoAnn E. Kitchel.
p. cm.
Summary: In January of 1924, a twenty-six-year-old pianist, George Gershwin,
finds himself slated to compose, in only five weeks, a concerto that defines "American music,"
and the result is his masterpiece, Rhapsody in Blue.
ISBN-13: 978-1-57091-556-7; ISBN-10: 1-57091-556-3 (reinforced for library use)
1. Gershwin, George, 1898–1937—Juvenile fiction. 2. Gershwin, George, 1898–1937 Rhapsody in blue—
Juvenile fiction. [1. Gershwin, George, 1898–1937—Fiction. 2. Gershwin, George, 1898–1937 Rhapsody in
blue—Fiction. 3. Composers—Fiction.] I. Kitchel, JoAnn E., ill. II. Title.
PZ7.C314Ger   2006
[E]—dc22   2005006009

Printed in Korea
(hc) 10 9 8 7

Illustrations done in watercolor and ink on Arches cold press paper
Display type and text type set in Parisian and Cochin
Color separations by KHL Chroma Graphics, Singapore
Printed February 2013 by Sung In Printing
in Gunpo-So, Kyonggi-Do, Korea
Production supervision by Brian G. Walker
Designed by Diane M. Earley

071315.3K1

For Mom. Written in memory of Frank M. Pollard, saxophonist with the Ted Weems Band and grandfather extraordinaire!
—A. H. C.

For Gary
—J. E. K.

This **PJ BOOK** belongs to

_____

_____

PJ Library®

JEWISH BEDTIME STORIES and SONGS

t was a Friday afternoon in early January 1924. George and Ira Gershwin were hanging out with B.G. "Buddy" DeSylva in a neighborhood pool hall on the Lower East Side. Ira sat by the window, reading the *New York Daily* while George and Buddy played pool.

"Hey, fellas! Listen to this," said Ira. "It sounds like our old pal Paul has come up with a new publicity scheme." He began to read aloud:

> In an attempt to determine "what is American music," orchestra leader Paul Whiteman is organizing a concert entitled "An Experiment in Modern Music." This concert will take place in Aeolian Hall on February 12 and will be attended by the world's musical elite.

George closed one eye, focusing on his shot. "Hmm," he mumbled distractedly.

"George, I think you better pay attention," said Ira. "You're gonna want to hear this next part."

Included on the program will be new compositions by local composers. George Gershwin is at work on a jazz concerto that will be featured in the concert.

George dropped his pool cue. "WHAT!?" he exclaimed. "Let me see that."

"It's all right there in black and white," chuckled Ira. "You better get to work, little brother. You've only got five weeks before the big show."

"This is crazy!" said George as he reached for his coat and hat. "Paul and I talked about working on some new music, but he never said anything about a concert. I've got to talk with him right away."

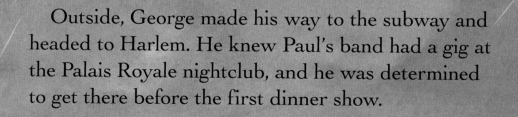

Outside, George made his way to the subway and headed to Harlem. He knew Paul's band had a gig at the Palais Royale nightclub, and he was determined to get there before the first dinner show.

"Hey, George, what a surprise," said Paul, seeing his friend walk through the backstage door. "Are you going to sit in with the band?"

"Not tonight," said George, shaking the rain from his hat. "I'm in no mood to play. What's this about me writing a piano concerto for a concert at Aeolian Hall?"

"You're looking a little steamed," said Paul. "How come?"

"How come?" replied George. "I just read in the paper that in a few weeks I am supposedly premiering a concerto that I haven't even started writing yet!"

A worried look crossed Paul's face. "Supposedly?" he asked. "Oh, George, don't tell me you're thinking about backing out. I need you on this concert. Your concerto is the highlight of the show."

"What concerto?" yelled George. "I haven't written a concerto! I wouldn't even know where to start! That's the whole problem. Don't you get it?"

Paul didn't respond right away. Instead, he motioned for his friend to sit down. Finally he said, "Look, George, if anyone can compose a concerto in a few weeks, you can. You're Manhattan's musical genius."

"I can't do it," said George.

"What kind of attitude is that?" asked Paul. "Of course you can! You've been playing classical music since you were twelve, plus you're one of the best song-pluggers ever to come out of Tin-Pan Alley."

"Yes, but . . ."

"But nothing," said Paul as he turned his friend's chair around to face one of the makeup mirrors. "Look at you! Twenty-six-year-old George Gershwin, composer of six Broadway shows with a new musical opening in Boston this month. Geez, George. You're a natural talent. What are you so worried about?"

"Vaudeville songs and Broadway medleys aren't the same thing as a concerto," explained George. "A concerto doesn't have words to hold it together—it's just the piano and the orchestra."

"But you're the best pianist I know," said Paul. "And as far as writing melodies go, I've never seen anyone make up a tune as fast as you. The music just flows from your fingertips."

George stared at his reflection for a moment. "You really think I can do it?" he asked.

"It'll be a piece of cake!" exclaimed Paul. "Just imagine you're Rachmaninov and then jazz it up a little. The crowds will love it!"

"Okay," said George as he straightened his tie and adjusted his hat. "If you think I can do it, then I'll give it a shot."

Filled with enthusiasm, George went straight home. He took out his father's new phonograph and stayed up late listening to concertos by Liszt and Chopin—great composers from the past.

"These will inspire me," he thought. But when he woke up the next morning, he couldn't think of a single new musical idea. He went to the piano and tried to improvise—nothing. He bought a fresh pack of paper and a new pen—nothing. He took a walk in Central Park—nothing. George tried everything to spark his creative energy, but nothing worked.

By the time Monday morning rolled around, he hadn't written a single note of his new concerto. Depressed, he packed his bags and made his way to the train station. He was heading to Boston to start rehearsals for his new musical.

"How could I have let Paul talk me into writing a concerto?" he mumbled to himself as he boarded the train. "I'll have to call him tonight and put an end to the whole silly idea."

As the train made its way north, George listened to the
wheels rocking against the tracks—rattlety, rattlety, bang,
rattlety, rattlety, bang. Soon his hands and feet began to
imitate the rhythm—clappety, clappety, tap, clappety,
clappety, tap.

George looked out the window and his mind began to
drift. At first the rhythm of the train reminded him of the
klezmer band at Ira's bar mitzvah years ago—clappety,
clappety, tap. He could almost hear the wailing strains of
the clarinet against the syncopated rhythm of the fiddle.

George's thoughts drifted to the Palais Royale: dancing the foxtrot, cheek to cheek, with a beautiful girl. Clappety, clappety, tap—the foxtrot reminded him of ragtime. He remembered roller-skating to the Barron Wilkins Club in Harlem. Since he was just a kid then, he was never allowed inside, so he sat on the curb and listened to the intoxicating rhythms and harmonies—clappety, clappety, tap—ragtime and the blues.

Maple Leaf Rag

Clappety, clappety, tap, clappety, clappety, tap. George listened to the rhythm of the train for a long time, and as he did, he got an idea about how he could write his concerto. "Instead of composing new melodies, I'll use the music that's already in my head," he thought. "Klezmer, foxtrot, ragtime, and blues. My concerto will be a tuneful kaleidoscope—a rhapsody about the music that surrounds me!"

In Boston George worked on the concerto whenever
he got the chance: before breakfast, during rehearsal
breaks, and late at night after the theater closed. He
thought about all the music he knew as a kid and tried
to find a place for it in his concerto. He also looked
through his tune book—a special music diary he kept
filled with melodies for new songs.
George put all his energy into
writing the concerto. When he
returned to New York two weeks
later, it was almost finished. He
played what he had written for
Ira and Buddy.

"It's got a little of everything," said Buddy.

"I'm impressed!" said Ira.

"Thanks," said George. "But it's not finished yet. Something's missing, but I can't figure out what. I've been concentrating so hard I can barely think."

"Too much work and not enough play," said Ira. "You need a break."

"Hey," said Buddy. "Ira and I are going to a swell party tonight on Madison Avenue. Why don't you tag along? It promises to be a real swanky affair."

The party was in a spacious new penthouse on top of a tall skyscraper. Large windows revealed a beautiful view of downtown. There was a grand piano in the middle of the room, and as usual, George was drawn to it like a bear to honey. He sat down and gazed out at the twinkling lights of Manhattan.

"Boy, did I miss this city!" he thought to himself. As he began to improvise, a marvelous melody rose from the piano. George listened carefully to the tune, and all at once, he realized he had found it—the missing theme for his concerto. "It's a love song for New York," he thought. "All that time in Boston almost made me forget."

George worked on his concerto for one more week. When it was finished, he showed it to his brother. "This is swell!" Ira exclaimed. "Has it got a title?"

"I was thinking of calling it *American Rhapsody*," replied George.

Ira thought for a moment. "That doesn't quite work," he said. "You need a name with more pep. Why not put a color in the title, like that artist Whistler does? He calls his paintings things like *Nocturne in Black and Gold* and *Arrangement in Gray and Black*."

"How about *Rhapsody in Blue*?" exclaimed George.

"That's it!" cried Ira. "*Rhapsody in Blue*, a concerto for piano and orchestra by George Gershwin."

Once a title had been found, George gave the concerto to Ferde Grofé, a friend who had agreed to write the parts for the orchestra. On February 4th the score was finished and rehearsals began. George had been asked to play the solo piano part, and every morning he practiced with Paul and the other musicians at the Palais Royale. Everyone worked hard to learn their parts. By February 12th they were ready for the big show.

When George approached Aeolian Hall an hour before the concert, he was shocked to see a huge crowd standing outside in the snow.

"The concert sold out hours ago," said Paul with excitement. "It looks like that newspaper article did the trick!"

"You've filled the seats," said George nervously. "Let's just hope they like the music."

George had good reason to worry. Although Paul had advertised the concert as "an experiment in modern music," there was nothing new about most of the program. Blues tunes, foxtrots, popular songs, and rags . . . except for a few short classical compositions, the music was nothing more than regular nightclub fare. As the concert progressed, the audience began to feel cheated. A few started to heckle the orchestra: "This isn't what you play in a concert hall!" Others stood up to leave.

Paul panicked. "George, get out there quick," he cried. "We need something new. Let's play your concerto before we have a riot on our hands!"

George dashed out on stage and took his seat at the piano. Paul walked out behind him and gave the orchestra its cue. All at once, the clarinet let out a wail that made the fleeing listeners stop dead in their tracks. They rushed back to their seats, and within seconds the klezmer howl was transformed into a sultry blues tune. The trombones joined in, followed by sassy trumpets and smooth violins.

Jazz mingled with classical virtuosity as George's fingers rushed up and down the keyboard. Like Scot Joplin and Rachmaninov rolled into one, he crossed his hands back and forth, wowing the audience with a fiery display. Klezmer, blues, ragtime, and foxtrot rose from the orchestra one after the other, blending with the piano into a musical melting pot. There was even a banjo thrown into the mix. Who knew a concerto could sound like this?

As the music progressed, the audience's enthusiasm only
increased. They swayed in their seats and bobbed their heads.
At times they could even hear a hint of George's inspirational
train—clappety, clappety, tap. It didn't seem the *Rhapsody* could
get much better, but then the violins and brass started playing
George's love song for New York.

The audience nearly exploded with joy. The theme was so expansive, so absolutely beautiful. It rose from the stage like a soaring skyscraper. George had somehow captured the spirit of modern life—the hustle-bustle rhythm and electric energy of Manhattan. *Rhapsody in Blue* marked a new direction for modern music. George had composed an American masterpiece.

Author's Note

Gershwin's Rhapsody in Blue is a true story. George and Ira Gershwin, Paul Whiteman, and B. G. DeSylva ("Buddy" to his friends) all worked in New York in the 1920s. George Gershwin (1898–1937) first found success in 1920 when he wrote a song called "Swanee," sung by Al Jolson, that hit the top of the charts. Gershwin also wrote music for Broadway, the movies, nightclubs, and concert halls—everything from jazz to opera arias. His most famous classical works include the opera *Porgy and Bess* and his jazz-infused concerto *Rhapsody in Blue*. The events in this book closely follow Gershwin's description of his inspiration for the concerto.

> . . . I had to appear in Boston for the premiere of *Sweet Little Devil* [with lyrics by B. G. DeSylva]. It was on the train, with its steely rhythms, its rattlety-bang that is so often stimulating to a composer, that I suddenly heard—even saw on paper—the complete construction of the Rhapsody, from beginning to end. No new themes came to me, but I worked on the thematic material already in my mind and tried to conceive of the composition as a whole. I heard it as sort of a musical kaleidoscope of America—of our vast melting pot, of our incomparable national pep, our blues, our metropolitan madness.[1]

George's older brother Ira claims to have come up with the final title. After viewing a painting by James McNeill Whistler called *Arrangement in Gray and Black* (better known as *Whistler's Mother*), Ira suggested a similar title for his brother's concerto. The title *Rhapsody in Blue* was born. The color blue is a reference to George's use of blue notes (notes added to the traditional musical scale that help give jazz its distinctive sound) throughout the piece.

There are many versions of *Rhapsody in Blue*. Gershwin revised the work on several occasions, and other composers (Ferde Grofé, Henry Levine, and Leonard Bernstein) also changed elements of the piece. In writing this book, I relied on the "commemorative facsimile edition" published by Warner Brothers in 1987, because this version comes closest to the score prepared for Whiteman's concert "An Experiment in Modern Music."

1. Merle Armitage, ed., *George Gershwin* (New York: Longmans, Green, & Co., 1938), 188.